NOTE TO PARENTS

Welcome to Kingfisher Readers! This program is designed to help young readers build skills, confidence, and a love of reading as they explore their favorite topics.

These tips can help you get more from the experience of reading books together. But remember, the most important thing is to make reading fun!

Tips to Warm Up Before Reading

- Ask your child to share what they already know about the topic.
- Preview the pages, pictures, sub-heads, and captions, so your reader will have an idea what is coming.
- Share your questions. What are you both wondering about?

While Reading

- Stop and think at the end of each section. What was that about?
- Let the words make pictures in your minds. Share what you see.
- When you see a new word, talk it over. What does it mean?
- Do you have more questions? Wonder out loud!

After Reading

- Share the parts that were most interesting or surprising.
- Make connections to other books, similar topics, or experiences.
- Discuss what you'd like to know more about. Then find out!

With five distinct levels and a wealth of appealing topics, the Kingfisher Readers series provides children with an exciting way to learn to read about the world around them. Enjoy!

Ellie Costa, M.S. Ed.
Literacy Specialist, Bank Street School for Children, New York

KINGFISHER READERS

level **4**

The Arctic and Antarctica

Philip Steele

KINGFISHER
NEW YORK

KINGFISHER
LONDON & NEW YORK

Copyright © Kingfisher 2013
Published in the United States by Kingfisher,
175 Fifth Ave., New York, NY 10010
Kingfisher is an imprint of Macmillan Children's Books, London.
All rights reserved.

Distributed in the U.S. and Canada by Macmillan,
175 Fifth Ave., New York, NY 10010

Library of Congress Cataloging-in-Publication data
has been applied for.

Series editor: Thea Feldman
Literacy consultant: Ellie Costa, Bank Street College, New York
Text for U.S. edition written by Thea Feldman

ISBN: 978-0-7534-7092-3 (HB)
ISBN: 978-0-7534-7093-0 (PB)

Kingfisher books are available for special promotions
and premiums. For details contact: Special Markets
Department, Macmillan, 175 Fifth Ave.,
New York, NY 10010.

For more information, please visit
www.kingfisherbooks.com

Printed in China
9 8 7 6 5 4 3 2 1
1TR/0713/WKT/UG/105MA

Picture credits
The Publisher would like to thank the following for permission to reproduce their material. Every care has
been taken to trace copyright holders. However, if there have been unintentional omissions or failure to trace
copyright holders, we apologize and will, if informed, endeavour to make corrections in any future edition.
Top = t; Bottom = b; Center = c; Left = l; Right = r
Cover Shutterstock/Gentoo Multimedia; Corbis/Robert van der Hilst; Pages 3t Getty/Martin Hartley;
3ct FLPA/Tui De Roy/Minden; 3c Corbis/Layne Kennedy; 3cb Frank Lane Picture Agency (FLPA)/David
Tipling; 3b FLPA/Jules Cox; 4 KF Archive; 5t KF Archive; 5b Shutterstock/Photodynamic; 6 Corbis/Alaska
Stock; 7 FLPA/Jules Cox; 8 Getty/OSF; 9t Alamy/All Canada Photos; 9b Shutterstock/Gary Whitton;
10 Corbis/Paul Souders; 11t FLPA/Norbert Wu/Minden; 11b FLPA/Patricio Robles/Minden; 12t Corbis/
Glen Bartley/All Canada Photos; 12b Alamy/Steven J. Kazlowski; 13t FLPA/David Tipling; 13b Corbis/
Steven J. Kazlowski; 14 Corbis/Layne Kennedy; 15t ArcticPhoto/Bryan & Cherry Alexander; 15b Corbis/
Michel Setbourn; 16 Getty/Imagno; 17t Corbis/Bettman; 17b Getty/Martin Hartley; 18 ArcticPhoto/Bryan
& Cherry Alexander; 19t Corbis/Thomas Pickard Photos; 19b Corbis/George Steinmetz; 20l FLPA/Flip
Nicklin/Minden; 20r KF Archive; 21t Shutterstock/nice_pictures; 21b FLPA/Tui De Roy/Minden;
22 KF Archive; 23t Corbis/Hulton; 23b Corbis/Reuters; 24t Corbis/Galen Rowell; 24b Corbis/Alfred
Wegener Institute/Hans-Christian Woeste; 25 KF Archive; 26 Corbis/George Steinmetz; 27 Corbis/Denis
Sinyakov; 28 ArcticPhoto/Bryan & Cherry Alexander; 29 FLPA/ Konrad Wothe/Imagebroker.

Contents

The ends of the Earth

If you travel very far to the north or south, you will reach the North Pole or the South Pole. These are very cold places that always have ice and snow. They are difficult places for people to survive.

The North Pole is the most northern point on Earth. It is not on land. It is in the Arctic Ocean. The North Pole is always frozen solid. The area surrounding the North Pole is called the Arctic. The Arctic includes parts of Canada, Russia, and many other places.

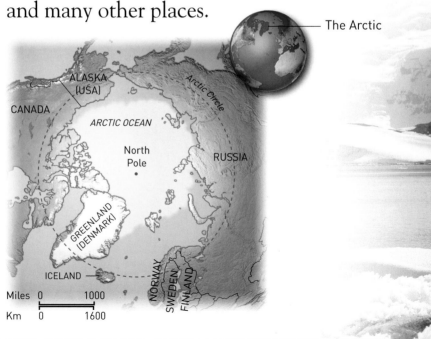

The Arctic

ALASKA (USA)

CANADA

ARCTIC OCEAN

Arctic Circle

North Pole

RUSSIA

GREENLAND (DENMARK)

ICELAND

NORWAY

SWEDEN

FINLAND

Miles 0   1000

Km   0   1600

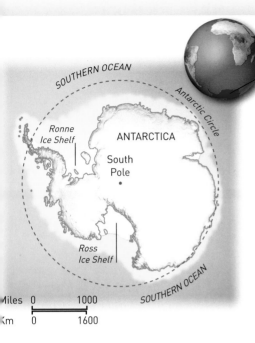

Antarctica

The South Pole is the most southern point on Earth. It is on land. It is on Antarctica. The South Pole is always frozen solid.

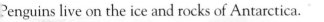

Penguins live on the ice and rocks of Antarctica.

The big freeze

When it is winter at one pole, it is summer at the other. Summers are short and can be warm in some areas. But most places have summer temperatures between 14°F (–10°C) and 50°F (10°C).

Winters are long and cold. Temperatures can drop below –58°F (–50°C)! New snow does not fall very often. Even so, there is a lot of snow on the ice. Strong winds stir up the snow, creating **blizzards**.

It is difficult to see anything during an Antarctic blizzard.

Just how cold can it get?

The world's lowest known temperature was recorded in Antarctica. At the Vostok scientific base on July 21, 1983, it was –128.2°F (–89°C)!

A group of walruses rest on an Arctic ice floe.

Sunshine at midnight

In the middle of the polar summer, it stays light even at night. In the middle of the polar winter, it stays dark all day long.

During winter at the poles, snow is not the only thing that moves. Ice moves too! Slabs of floating sea ice, called **ice floes**, form. **Icebergs** form too. Icebergs are pieces of **glaciers** and **ice shelves** that break off and float in the water. Icebergs can be the size of mountains.

7

Land in the Arctic

The land around the Arctic Ocean is covered by ice and snow in the winter. In the summer, the ice and snow melt. You can see the surface of the ground again. But the soil beneath the surface always stays frozen. This type of land is called **tundra**.

There are no trees growing on the tundra. That is because a tree's roots need to grow long and take a firm hold of deep soil. They cannot take hold of frozen soil.

On top of the world

The most northern patch of land on Earth is an island called Kaffeklubben, in Greenland.

Icy mountains covered by snow on the coast of Greenland

Some plants can grow in the tundra's soil. In the summer, there are bright wildflowers. There are green grasses and mosses too. These plants do not have roots that need deep soil in order to grow.

Forests filled with trees such as spruce and fir are located south of the tundra.

Animals in the Arctic Ocean

All kinds of animals live in the Arctic Ocean. They have found ways to survive in the bitter cold. The ocean is full of tiny plants and animals, called **plankton**. Plankton provides a rich food for many fish and whales. Seabirds cruise above the water and catch the fish.

Cod survival

Arctic cod can survive in colder waters than any other fish. Their bodies produce chemicals that prevent them from freezing. It is like the antifreeze that keeps our cars running in the winter!

A humpback whale leaps out of the water.

Seals are at home in the cold water. They mostly feed on fish. Their streamlined bodies help them swim. Thick layers of **blubber** keep them warm.

Seals need to come up to the surface to breathe air. There may be a hungry polar bear waiting for them above the ice! The polar bear is the top hunter in the Arctic. It is a powerful swimmer and hunts on ice floes as well as along the coast of the tundra.

A polar bear catches a seal.

Animals on the tundra

The tundra is busiest in the summer. Insects come to eat the colorful wildflowers. Little birds come to eat the insects. Snow geese fly in from the south. They come for the warm weather and to feed on the fresh grasses.

Whimbrels (left) use their long, curved bills to feed on insects, worms, and crabs.

Snow geese leave the tundra every winter and return for the summer.

When winter comes, many animals leave for warmer places. Some stay, such as the arctic fox and its prey, the arctic hare. Their coats change color with the seasons. This helps them blend in to their surroundings and be hidden. In the winter, their coats are white like the snow. In warmer months, their coats match the ground and rocks.

The arctic fox's winter coat

A long journey

In North America wild reindeer, called caribou, leave the Arctic each winter and return in the spring (see below). Some herds can number in the hundreds of thousands. They can travel up to 3,000 miles (5,000 kilometers) roundtrip.

Peoples of the Arctic

People settled in the Arctic thousands of years ago. They learned how to survive the harsh climate. They wore animal skins and furs to keep warm. They became experts at fishing and at hunting seals too.

An Inuit hunter with his team of dogs

The **Inuit** people of North America traveled in boats called **kayaks** or by dog sled. They built houses of stone and earth. Using blocks of snow, they also built shelters we call **igloos**. In the far north of Europe and Asia, peoples such as the Saami and the Nenets often herded reindeer for a living.

These Inuit
girls enjoy a
snowmobile ride.

Some people in the Arctic still live the same way
as their **ancestors** did. Others live more modern
lives. They travel by snowmobiles or planes.
They live in modern villages with modern homes
and stores. Still other people have moved away
to cities, for work and other reasons.

Arctic fun

Reindeer herders such as the
Saami and the Nenets like to
hold spring festivals. These may
include competitions such as
reindeer racing, reindeer roping,
and snowmobile races.

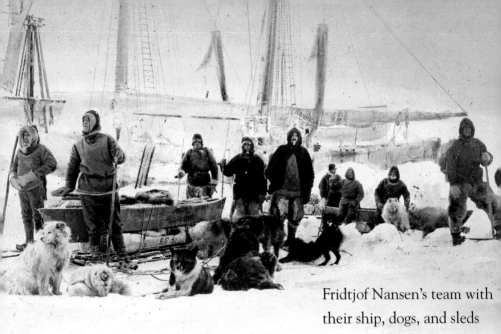

Fridtjof Nansen's team with their ship, dogs, and sleds

Arctic explorers

The **Vikings** were the first known people to explore the Arctic. They settled in Iceland and southern Greenland over a thousand years ago. Hundreds of years later, different explorers tried to reach the North Pole.

In the 1890s, a Norwegian explorer named Fridtjof Nansen tried to reach the Arctic by ship. His ship, the *Fram*, hit floating ice. Nansen and another crewmember tried to keep going on skis! But there was too much drifting ice, so they had to turn back. They returned home three years after they set out!

Robert Peary was an American who tried to reach the North Pole on three separate trips.

Frederick Cook claimed to be the first person to reach the North Pole in 1908. But in 1909 many people believed Robert Peary was first. Back then it was hard to show proof, so it's not clear who was first.

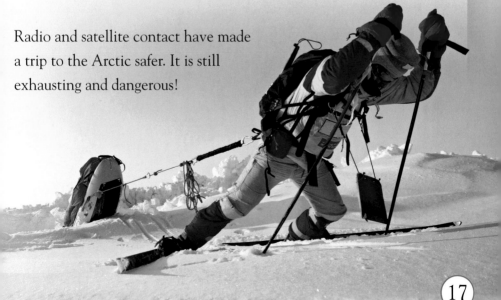

Radio and satellite contact have made a trip to the Arctic safer. It is still exhausting and dangerous!

South to Antarctica

Antarctica is a **continent**. Almost all of Antarctica's land is covered by one vast sheet of ice. The ice is more than 1 mile (2 kilometers) thick on average. Antarctica's ice sheet makes up 90 percent of all the ice—and more than 60 percent of all the fresh water—on our planet!

Antarctica is also the world's largest desert! Deserts get less than 10 inches (25 centimeters) of rain or snow a year. And it's usually too cold in Antarctica for much new rain or snow to fall.

The Antarctic desert has some jagged mountain ranges.

Glaciers extend out to sea, forming ice shelves along the coast.

Antarctica has a small tundra, compared to the one in the Arctic. Mosses and **lichens** are among the few plants that can survive there.

Ice and fire

Mount Erebus on Ross Island near Antarctica is an active volcano. It spews out hot gases and lava. The heat creates caves and smoking towers in the ice.

Animals in Antarctica

Few animals can survive in Antarctica. Inland there is thick ice and a lack of plants and other food. Life is only possible around the coasts and ice shelves.

The Southern Ocean is a rich source of food. Small, shrimplike animals called krill eat plankton. The blue whale, the biggest animal on Earth, gulps down tons of krill every day.

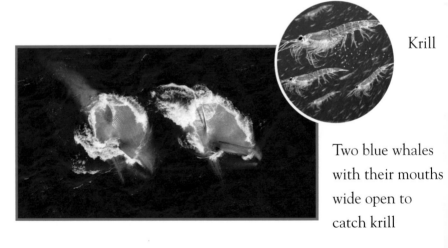

Krill

Two blue whales with their mouths wide open to catch krill

The colossal squid is another giant of the Southern Ocean. It can grow to be 46 feet (14 meters) long. Weddell seals live on the ice shelf. They feed on fish, squid, and krill.

A small bird called the arctic tern travels between the Arctic and Antarctica each year. It flies a total of about 44,000 miles (71,000 kilometers). It makes the longest journey of any animal.

Five kinds of penguins live in Antarctica. They spend most of the time in the water. They breed, nest, and raise chicks on shore. In the water they face danger from killer whales and leopard seals. On shore, eggs and chicks face attacks from seabirds such as the skua.

These Emperor penguins gather on land in large groups called colonies.

Antarctic explorers

Russian, British, and American sailors first saw the shores of Antarctica in the 1820s. In 1853, Nathaniel Palmer, a seal hunter, became the first American to land there.

In 1910, a Norwegian explorer named Roald Amundsen sailed to the Antarctic coast. On December 14, 1911, 57 days after setting out from the coast, Amundsen became the first person to reach the South Pole.

Amundsen's team used dog sleds and skis to travel quickly over snow and glacier ice.

Scott arrived in Antarctica in 1911. Scott wrote in his diary: "Great God! This is an awful place!"

A team of British explorers led by Robert Falcon Scott arrived at the South Pole after the Norwegians, in January 1912. Scott was disappointed not to have arrived first. On the return journey there were terrible blizzards. All the British explorers died of cold and hunger.

Scott's hut

The hut set up and used by Scott during his trip is still standing in Antarctica. Some of the food and other items have stayed frozen for more than 100 years!

Today, travelers to Antarctica have modern equipment and better support. Even some tourists take trips to Antarctica during the summer months.

Research stations

The mainland of Antarctica does not belong to any one nation. There are strict limits on who can visit and what they can do there.

International flags surround the marker post at the South Pole.

Thirty countries have research stations on Antarctica. No one lives there permanently because of the harsh conditions. But scientists stay at the stations for months at a time. The stations are designed to withstand extreme cold and winds up to 186 miles (300 kilometers) an hour.

This German research station, called Neumayer III, opened in 2009.

Scientists study Antarctica because they believe what happens there affects the rest of the world. They study the weather. They study the air, which is the least polluted air on the planet. They measure the thickness of the ice sheet and the size of the ice shelf. They study the rocks, the plants, and the coastal animals too.

Scientists have tools to check their exact location in the Antarctic desert.

Changing climate

Scientists studying ice and weather at the poles warn us that the climate in these places is changing quickly. Ice sheets are becoming thinner. The sea ice is melting. It is getting warmer and warmer.

Climate clues

Scientists can find out what the climate has been like over the last 500,000 years in Antarctica! They get the answers by drilling out sheet ice from more than 2 miles (3,700 meters) down.

The mining city of Norilsk, in the Russian Arctic,
is one of the most polluted places in the world.

The climate is getting warmer in the rest of the
world too. Most scientists think human activity
is responsible for how quickly this is happening.
People burn fuel and use other things that send
gases into the air. The gases form a layer around
Earth that traps heat and makes the planet warmer.

A big meltdown at the poles could cause low
islands and coasts to be flooded all around the
world. Places would be destroyed and many
lives lost.

An Inuit
hunter out on
the ice

The future

The Arctic and Antarctica have gotten warmer
in the last 100 years. If the climate keeps
getting warmer, many changes will happen in
these places. If the ice keeps melting, animals
such as polar bears and walruses in the Arctic,
and penguins in Antarctica, will all struggle
to survive. Peoples of the Arctic will also have
trouble continuing to live as they do now.

There are other changes that could happen in
the Arctic. Valuable **minerals** and oil are deep
inside the ground. Mining and oil companies
want to dig and drill in the Arctic to get to the
minerals and oil. It would change the look of
the Arctic and life there forever.

Boats beat the ice

For hundreds of years, explorers tried to find sailing routes around the edges of the Arctic Ocean. They were always beaten by the ice and many lost their lives. But by 2010, there was so little sea ice left that two boats managed to complete the voyage.

Antarctica has minerals in the ground too. But in 1961 it became an international refuge. No one can drill there. But climate change is still a concern. People in every part of the world need to do all they can to slow down climate change. If people use less fuel and power, they can help keep the poles wild, beautiful, and cold.

Glossary

ancestors a person's relatives who lived a very long time ago

blizzard a severe snowstorm with high winds that tosses snow around, making it hard to see

blubber a layer of fat that protects some animals, such as whales, seals, and polar bears, from the cold

climate the typical weather conditions in a place over a long period of time

continent one of the world's seven largest masses of land

glacier a slow moving river of ice and snow formed at the poles

ice floe a sheet of ice floating in a sea or river

ice shelf a wide and thick piece of ice that forms where a glacier meets the ocean

iceberg a large block of ice that has broken off from a glacier or ice shelf

igloo a round shelter made from blocks of frozen snow, used by Inuit hunters

Inuit people whose families have lived in parts of the Arctic since very early times

kayak a lightweight canoe for one or two people using a pole with paddles at both ends

lichens gray, green, or yellow plants that grow in flat patches on rocks

minerals natural things we mine from or dig out of the earth and use, such as natural gas and coal

mosses nonflowering green plants with short stems

plankton tiny plants and animals that float in the ocean

polluted dirty and unhealthy

refuge a place that is protected from being changed or damaged

tundra an open region of the Arctic or Antarctica with very few trees. Tundra is frozen in the winter, but the soil on the surface melts in the summer

Vikings seafaring people who lived in Denmark, Sweden, and Norway from the A.D. 700s to around the 1000s

Index

If you have enjoyed reading
this book, look out for more in
the Kingfisher Readers series!

Collect
and read
them all!

For a full list of Kingfisher Readers books, plus
guidance for teachers and parents and activities
and fun stuff for kids, go to the Kingfisher Readers
website: **www.kingfisherreaders.com**